This Belongs to

NAME:	
ADDRESS:	
PHONE:	

___ / ___ / ___   TO   ___ / ___ / ___

START / END DATES

Mood Tracker

MONTH							WEEK		

	MONDAY	TUESDAY	WEDNESDAY	THURSDAY	FRIDAY	SATURDAY	SUNDAY
HAPPY							
NEUTRAL							
SAD							

DAY	EMOTION	WHAT HAPPENED?	DAILY SCORE
MONDAY			☆ ☆ ☆ ☆ ☆
TUESDAY			☆ ☆ ☆ ☆ ☆
WEDNESDAY			☆ ☆ ☆ ☆ ☆
THURSDAY			☆ ☆ ☆ ☆ ☆
FRIDAY			☆ ☆ ☆ ☆ ☆
SATURDAY			☆ ☆ ☆ ☆ ☆
SUNDAY			☆ ☆ ☆ ☆ ☆

Notes

Mood Tracker

MONTH						WEEK			
HAPPY									
NEUTRAL									
SAD									
	MONDAY	TUESDAY	WEDNESDAY	THURSDAY		FRIDAY	SATURDAY		SUNDAY

DAY	EMOTION	WHAT HAPPENED?	DAILY SCORE
MONDAY			☆ ☆ ☆ ☆ ☆
TUESDAY			☆ ☆ ☆ ☆ ☆
WEDNESDAY			☆ ☆ ☆ ☆ ☆
THURSDAY			☆ ☆ ☆ ☆ ☆
FRIDAY			☆ ☆ ☆ ☆ ☆
SATURDAY			☆ ☆ ☆ ☆ ☆
SUNDAY			☆ ☆ ☆ ☆ ☆

Notes

Mood Tracker

MONTH						WEEK			
HAPPY									
NEUTRAL									
SAD									
	MONDAY	TUESDAY	WEDNESDAY	THURSDAY	FRIDAY		SATURDAY	SUNDAY	

DAY	EMOTION	WHAT HAPPENED?	DAILY SCORE
MONDAY			☆ ☆ ☆ ☆ ☆
TUESDAY			☆ ☆ ☆ ☆ ☆
WEDNESDAY			☆ ☆ ☆ ☆ ☆
THURSDAY			☆ ☆ ☆ ☆ ☆
FRIDAY			☆ ☆ ☆ ☆ ☆
SATURDAY			☆ ☆ ☆ ☆ ☆
SUNDAY			☆ ☆ ☆ ☆ ☆

Notes

Mood Tracker

MONTH		WEEK	

	MONDAY	TUESDAY	WEDNESDAY	THURSDAY	FRIDAY	SATURDAY	SUNDAY
HAPPY							
NEUTRAL							
SAD							

DAY	EMOTION	WHAT HAPPENED?	DAILY SCORE
MONDAY			☆ ☆ ☆ ☆ ☆
TUESDAY			☆ ☆ ☆ ☆ ☆
WEDNESDAY			☆ ☆ ☆ ☆ ☆
THURSDAY			☆ ☆ ☆ ☆ ☆
FRIDAY			☆ ☆ ☆ ☆ ☆
SATURDAY			☆ ☆ ☆ ☆ ☆
SUNDAY			☆ ☆ ☆ ☆ ☆

Notes

Mood Tracker

MONTH		WEEK	

HAPPY							
NEUTRAL							
SAD							
	MONDAY	TUESDAY	WEDNESDAY	THURSDAY	FRIDAY	SATURDAY	SUNDAY

DAY	EMOTION	WHAT HAPPENED?	DAILY SCORE
MONDAY			☆ ☆ ☆ ☆ ☆
TUESDAY			☆ ☆ ☆ ☆ ☆
WEDNESDAY			☆ ☆ ☆ ☆ ☆
THURSDAY			☆ ☆ ☆ ☆ ☆
FRIDAY			☆ ☆ ☆ ☆ ☆
SATURDAY			☆ ☆ ☆ ☆ ☆
SUNDAY			☆ ☆ ☆ ☆ ☆

Notes

Mood Tracker

MONTH		WEEK	

	MONDAY	TUESDAY	WEDNESDAY	THURSDAY	FRIDAY	SATURDAY	SUNDAY
HAPPY							
NEUTRAL							
SAD							

DAY	EMOTION	WHAT HAPPENED?	DAILY SCORE
MONDAY			☆ ☆ ☆ ☆ ☆
TUESDAY			☆ ☆ ☆ ☆ ☆
WEDNESDAY			☆ ☆ ☆ ☆ ☆
THURSDAY			☆ ☆ ☆ ☆ ☆
FRIDAY			☆ ☆ ☆ ☆ ☆
SATURDAY			☆ ☆ ☆ ☆ ☆
SUNDAY			☆ ☆ ☆ ☆ ☆

Notes

Mood Tracker

MONTH							WEEK		
HAPPY									
NEUTRAL									
SAD									
	MONDAY	TUESDAY	WEDNESDAY	THURSDAY	FRIDAY	SATURDAY	SUNDAY		

DAY	EMOTION	WHAT HAPPENED?	DAILY SCORE
MONDAY			☆ ☆ ☆ ☆ ☆
TUESDAY			☆ ☆ ☆ ☆ ☆
WEDNESDAY			☆ ☆ ☆ ☆ ☆
THURSDAY			☆ ☆ ☆ ☆ ☆
FRIDAY			☆ ☆ ☆ ☆ ☆
SATURDAY			☆ ☆ ☆ ☆ ☆
SUNDAY			☆ ☆ ☆ ☆ ☆

Notes

Mood Tracker

MONTH		WEEK	

	MONDAY	TUESDAY	WEDNESDAY	THURSDAY	FRIDAY	SATURDAY	SUNDAY
HAPPY							
NEUTRAL							
SAD							

DAY	EMOTION	WHAT HAPPENED?	DAILY SCORE
MONDAY			☆ ☆ ☆ ☆ ☆
TUESDAY			☆ ☆ ☆ ☆ ☆
WEDNESDAY			☆ ☆ ☆ ☆ ☆
THURSDAY			☆ ☆ ☆ ☆ ☆
FRIDAY			☆ ☆ ☆ ☆ ☆
SATURDAY			☆ ☆ ☆ ☆ ☆
SUNDAY			☆ ☆ ☆ ☆ ☆

Notes

Mood Tracker

MONTH							WEEK		
HAPPY									
NEUTRAL									
SAD									
	MONDAY	TUESDAY	WEDNESDAY	THURSDAY	FRIDAY	SATURDAY	SUNDAY		

DAY	EMOTION	WHAT HAPPENED?	DAILY SCORE
MONDAY			☆ ☆ ☆ ☆ ☆
TUESDAY			☆ ☆ ☆ ☆ ☆
WEDNESDAY			☆ ☆ ☆ ☆ ☆
THURSDAY			☆ ☆ ☆ ☆ ☆
FRIDAY			☆ ☆ ☆ ☆ ☆
SATURDAY			☆ ☆ ☆ ☆ ☆
SUNDAY			☆ ☆ ☆ ☆ ☆

Notes

Mood Tracker

MONTH					WEEK			
HAPPY								
NEUTRAL								
SAD								
	MONDAY	TUESDAY	WEDNESDAY	THURSDAY	FRIDAY	SATURDAY	SUNDAY	

DAY	EMOTION	WHAT HAPPENED?	DAILY SCORE
MONDAY			☆☆☆☆☆
TUESDAY			☆☆☆☆☆
WEDNESDAY			☆☆☆☆☆
THURSDAY			☆☆☆☆☆
FRIDAY			☆☆☆☆☆
SATURDAY			☆☆☆☆☆
SUNDAY			☆☆☆☆☆

Notes

Mood Tracker

MONTH		WEEK	

	MONDAY	TUESDAY	WEDNESDAY	THURSDAY	FRIDAY	SATURDAY	SUNDAY
HAPPY							
NEUTRAL							
SAD							

DAY	EMOTION	WHAT HAPPENED?	DAILY SCORE
MONDAY			☆ ☆ ☆ ☆ ☆
TUESDAY			☆ ☆ ☆ ☆ ☆
WEDNESDAY			☆ ☆ ☆ ☆ ☆
THURSDAY			☆ ☆ ☆ ☆ ☆
FRIDAY			☆ ☆ ☆ ☆ ☆
SATURDAY			☆ ☆ ☆ ☆ ☆
SUNDAY			☆ ☆ ☆ ☆ ☆

Notes

Mood Tracker

MONTH					WEEK			

	MONDAY	TUESDAY	WEDNESDAY	THURSDAY	FRIDAY	SATURDAY	SUNDAY
HAPPY							
NEUTRAL							
SAD							

DAY	EMOTION	WHAT HAPPENED?	DAILY SCORE
MONDAY			☆ ☆ ☆ ☆ ☆
TUESDAY			☆ ☆ ☆ ☆ ☆
WEDNESDAY			☆ ☆ ☆ ☆ ☆
THURSDAY			☆ ☆ ☆ ☆ ☆
FRIDAY			☆ ☆ ☆ ☆ ☆
SATURDAY			☆ ☆ ☆ ☆ ☆
SUNDAY			☆ ☆ ☆ ☆ ☆

Notes

Mood Tracker

MONTH						WEEK		

HAPPY								
NEUTRAL								
SAD								
	MONDAY	TUESDAY	WEDNESDAY	THURSDAY	FRIDAY	SATURDAY	SUNDAY	

DAY	EMOTION	WHAT HAPPENED?	DAILY SCORE
MONDAY			☆ ☆ ☆ ☆ ☆
TUESDAY			☆ ☆ ☆ ☆ ☆
WEDNESDAY			☆ ☆ ☆ ☆ ☆
THURSDAY			☆ ☆ ☆ ☆ ☆
FRIDAY			☆ ☆ ☆ ☆ ☆
SATURDAY			☆ ☆ ☆ ☆ ☆
SUNDAY			☆ ☆ ☆ ☆ ☆

Notes

Mood Tracker

MONTH		WEEK	

	MONDAY	TUESDAY	WEDNESDAY	THURSDAY	FRIDAY	SATURDAY	SUNDAY
HAPPY							
NEUTRAL							
SAD							

DAY	EMOTION	WHAT HAPPENED?	DAILY SCORE
MONDAY			☆ ☆ ☆ ☆ ☆
TUESDAY			☆ ☆ ☆ ☆ ☆
WEDNESDAY			☆ ☆ ☆ ☆ ☆
THURSDAY			☆ ☆ ☆ ☆ ☆
FRIDAY			☆ ☆ ☆ ☆ ☆
SATURDAY			☆ ☆ ☆ ☆ ☆
SUNDAY			☆ ☆ ☆ ☆ ☆

Notes

Mood Tracker

MONTH						WEEK		
HAPPY								
NEUTRAL								
SAD								
	MONDAY	TUESDAY	WEDNESDAY	THURSDAY	FRIDAY	SATURDAY	SUNDAY	

DAY	EMOTION	WHAT HAPPENED?	DAILY SCORE
MONDAY			☆ ☆ ☆ ☆ ☆
TUESDAY			☆ ☆ ☆ ☆ ☆
WEDNESDAY			☆ ☆ ☆ ☆ ☆
THURSDAY			☆ ☆ ☆ ☆ ☆
FRIDAY			☆ ☆ ☆ ☆ ☆
SATURDAY			☆ ☆ ☆ ☆ ☆
SUNDAY			☆ ☆ ☆ ☆ ☆

Notes

Mood Tracker

MONTH							WEEK		
HAPPY									
NEUTRAL									
SAD									
	MONDAY	TUESDAY	WEDNESDAY	THURSDAY	FRIDAY	SATURDAY	SUNDAY		

DAY	EMOTION	WHAT HAPPENED?	DAILY SCORE
MONDAY			☆ ☆ ☆ ☆ ☆
TUESDAY			☆ ☆ ☆ ☆ ☆
WEDNESDAY			☆ ☆ ☆ ☆ ☆
THURSDAY			☆ ☆ ☆ ☆ ☆
FRIDAY			☆ ☆ ☆ ☆ ☆
SATURDAY			☆ ☆ ☆ ☆ ☆
SUNDAY			☆ ☆ ☆ ☆ ☆

Notes

Mood Tracker

MONTH		WEEK	

	MONDAY	TUESDAY	WEDNESDAY	THURSDAY	FRIDAY	SATURDAY	SUNDAY
HAPPY							
NEUTRAL							
SAD							

DAY	EMOTION	WHAT HAPPENED?	DAILY SCORE
MONDAY			☆ ☆ ☆ ☆ ☆
TUESDAY			☆ ☆ ☆ ☆ ☆
WEDNESDAY			☆ ☆ ☆ ☆ ☆
THURSDAY			☆ ☆ ☆ ☆ ☆
FRIDAY			☆ ☆ ☆ ☆ ☆
SATURDAY			☆ ☆ ☆ ☆ ☆
SUNDAY			☆ ☆ ☆ ☆ ☆

Notes

Mood Tracker

MONTH		WEEK	

	MONDAY	TUESDAY	WEDNESDAY	THURSDAY	FRIDAY	SATURDAY	SUNDAY
HAPPY							
NEUTRAL							
SAD							

DAY	EMOTION	WHAT HAPPENED?	DAILY SCORE
MONDAY			☆☆☆☆☆
TUESDAY			☆☆☆☆☆
WEDNESDAY			☆☆☆☆☆
THURSDAY			☆☆☆☆☆
FRIDAY			☆☆☆☆☆
SATURDAY			☆☆☆☆☆
SUNDAY			☆☆☆☆☆

Notes

Mood Tracker

MONTH		WEEK	

	MONDAY	TUESDAY	WEDNESDAY	THURSDAY	FRIDAY	SATURDAY	SUNDAY
HAPPY							
NEUTRAL							
SAD							

DAY	EMOTION	WHAT HAPPENED?	DAILY SCORE
MONDAY			☆ ☆ ☆ ☆ ☆
TUESDAY			☆ ☆ ☆ ☆ ☆
WEDNESDAY			☆ ☆ ☆ ☆ ☆
THURSDAY			☆ ☆ ☆ ☆ ☆
FRIDAY			☆ ☆ ☆ ☆ ☆
SATURDAY			☆ ☆ ☆ ☆ ☆
SUNDAY			☆ ☆ ☆ ☆ ☆

Notes

Mood Tracker

MONTH		WEEK	

	MONDAY	TUESDAY	WEDNESDAY	THURSDAY	FRIDAY	SATURDAY	SUNDAY
HAPPY							
NEUTRAL							
SAD							

DAY	EMOTION	WHAT HAPPENED?	DAILY SCORE
MONDAY			☆ ☆ ☆ ☆ ☆
TUESDAY			☆ ☆ ☆ ☆ ☆
WEDNESDAY			☆ ☆ ☆ ☆ ☆
THURSDAY			☆ ☆ ☆ ☆ ☆
FRIDAY			☆ ☆ ☆ ☆ ☆
SATURDAY			☆ ☆ ☆ ☆ ☆
SUNDAY			☆ ☆ ☆ ☆ ☆

Notes

Mood Tracker

MONTH		WEEK	

	MONDAY	TUESDAY	WEDNESDAY	THURSDAY	FRIDAY	SATURDAY	SUNDAY
HAPPY							
NEUTRAL							
SAD							

DAY	EMOTION	WHAT HAPPENED?	DAILY SCORE
MONDAY			☆ ☆ ☆ ☆ ☆
TUESDAY			☆ ☆ ☆ ☆ ☆
WEDNESDAY			☆ ☆ ☆ ☆ ☆
THURSDAY			☆ ☆ ☆ ☆ ☆
FRIDAY			☆ ☆ ☆ ☆ ☆
SATURDAY			☆ ☆ ☆ ☆ ☆
SUNDAY			☆ ☆ ☆ ☆ ☆

Notes

Mood Tracker

MONTH		WEEK	

	MONDAY	TUESDAY	WEDNESDAY	THURSDAY	FRIDAY	SATURDAY	SUNDAY
HAPPY							
NEUTRAL							
SAD							

DAY	EMOTION	WHAT HAPPENED?	DAILY SCORE
MONDAY			☆ ☆ ☆ ☆ ☆
TUESDAY			☆ ☆ ☆ ☆ ☆
WEDNESDAY			☆ ☆ ☆ ☆ ☆
THURSDAY			☆ ☆ ☆ ☆ ☆
FRIDAY			☆ ☆ ☆ ☆ ☆
SATURDAY			☆ ☆ ☆ ☆ ☆
SUNDAY			☆ ☆ ☆ ☆ ☆

Notes

Mood Tracker

MONTH		WEEK	

	MONDAY	TUESDAY	WEDNESDAY	THURSDAY	FRIDAY	SATURDAY	SUNDAY
HAPPY							
NEUTRAL							
SAD							

DAY	EMOTION	WHAT HAPPENED?	DAILY SCORE
MONDAY			☆☆☆☆☆
TUESDAY			☆☆☆☆☆
WEDNESDAY			☆☆☆☆☆
THURSDAY			☆☆☆☆☆
FRIDAY			☆☆☆☆☆
SATURDAY			☆☆☆☆☆
SUNDAY			☆☆☆☆☆

Notes

Mood Tracker

MONTH							WEEK		

HAPPY									
NEUTRAL									
SAD									
	MONDAY	TUESDAY	WEDNESDAY	THURSDAY	FRIDAY	SATURDAY	SUNDAY		

DAY	EMOTION	WHAT HAPPENED?	DAILY SCORE
MONDAY			☆ ☆ ☆ ☆ ☆
TUESDAY			☆ ☆ ☆ ☆ ☆
WEDNESDAY			☆ ☆ ☆ ☆ ☆
THURSDAY			☆ ☆ ☆ ☆ ☆
FRIDAY			☆ ☆ ☆ ☆ ☆
SATURDAY			☆ ☆ ☆ ☆ ☆
SUNDAY			☆ ☆ ☆ ☆ ☆

Notes

Mood Tracker

MONTH		WEEK	

	MONDAY	TUESDAY	WEDNESDAY	THURSDAY	FRIDAY	SATURDAY	SUNDAY
HAPPY							
NEUTRAL							
SAD							

DAY	EMOTION	WHAT HAPPENED?	DAILY SCORE
MONDAY			☆☆☆☆☆
TUESDAY			☆☆☆☆☆
WEDNESDAY			☆☆☆☆☆
THURSDAY			☆☆☆☆☆
FRIDAY			☆☆☆☆☆
SATURDAY			☆☆☆☆☆
SUNDAY			☆☆☆☆☆

Notes

Mood Tracker

MONTH		WEEK	

	MONDAY	TUESDAY	WEDNESDAY	THURSDAY	FRIDAY	SATURDAY	SUNDAY
HAPPY							
NEUTRAL							
SAD							

DAY	EMOTION	WHAT HAPPENED?	DAILY SCORE
MONDAY			☆ ☆ ☆ ☆ ☆
TUESDAY			☆ ☆ ☆ ☆ ☆
WEDNESDAY			☆ ☆ ☆ ☆ ☆
THURSDAY			☆ ☆ ☆ ☆ ☆
FRIDAY			☆ ☆ ☆ ☆ ☆
SATURDAY			☆ ☆ ☆ ☆ ☆
SUNDAY			☆ ☆ ☆ ☆ ☆

Notes

Mood Tracker

MONTH		WEEK	

	MONDAY	TUESDAY	WEDNESDAY	THURSDAY	FRIDAY	SATURDAY	SUNDAY
HAPPY							
NEUTRAL							
SAD							

DAY	EMOTION	WHAT HAPPENED?	DAILY SCORE
MONDAY			☆☆☆☆☆
TUESDAY			☆☆☆☆☆
WEDNESDAY			☆☆☆☆☆
THURSDAY			☆☆☆☆☆
FRIDAY			☆☆☆☆☆
SATURDAY			☆☆☆☆☆
SUNDAY			☆☆☆☆☆

Notes

Mood Tracker

MONTH		WEEK	

	MONDAY	TUESDAY	WEDNESDAY	THURSDAY	FRIDAY	SATURDAY	SUNDAY
HAPPY							
NEUTRAL							
SAD							

DAY	EMOTION	WHAT HAPPENED?	DAILY SCORE
MONDAY			☆ ☆ ☆ ☆ ☆
TUESDAY			☆ ☆ ☆ ☆ ☆
WEDNESDAY			☆ ☆ ☆ ☆ ☆
THURSDAY			☆ ☆ ☆ ☆ ☆
FRIDAY			☆ ☆ ☆ ☆ ☆
SATURDAY			☆ ☆ ☆ ☆ ☆
SUNDAY			☆ ☆ ☆ ☆ ☆

Notes

Mood Tracker

MONTH		WEEK	

	MONDAY	TUESDAY	WEDNESDAY	THURSDAY	FRIDAY	SATURDAY	SUNDAY
HAPPY							
NEUTRAL							
SAD							

DAY	EMOTION	WHAT HAPPENED?	DAILY SCORE
MONDAY			☆☆☆☆☆
TUESDAY			☆☆☆☆☆
WEDNESDAY			☆☆☆☆☆
THURSDAY			☆☆☆☆☆
FRIDAY			☆☆☆☆☆
SATURDAY			☆☆☆☆☆
SUNDAY			☆☆☆☆☆

Notes

Mood Tracker

MONTH		WEEK	

HAPPY									
NEUTRAL									
SAD									
	MONDAY	TUESDAY	WEDNESDAY	THURSDAY	FRIDAY	SATURDAY	SUNDAY		

DAY	EMOTION	WHAT HAPPENED?	DAILY SCORE
MONDAY			☆ ☆ ☆ ☆ ☆
TUESDAY			☆ ☆ ☆ ☆ ☆
WEDNESDAY			☆ ☆ ☆ ☆ ☆
THURSDAY			☆ ☆ ☆ ☆ ☆
FRIDAY			☆ ☆ ☆ ☆ ☆
SATURDAY			☆ ☆ ☆ ☆ ☆
SUNDAY			☆ ☆ ☆ ☆ ☆

Notes

Mood Tracker

MONTH		WEEK	

	MONDAY	TUESDAY	WEDNESDAY	THURSDAY	FRIDAY	SATURDAY	SUNDAY
HAPPY							
NEUTRAL							
SAD							

DAY	EMOTION	WHAT HAPPENED?	DAILY SCORE
MONDAY			☆ ☆ ☆ ☆ ☆
TUESDAY			☆ ☆ ☆ ☆ ☆
WEDNESDAY			☆ ☆ ☆ ☆ ☆
THURSDAY			☆ ☆ ☆ ☆ ☆
FRIDAY			☆ ☆ ☆ ☆ ☆
SATURDAY			☆ ☆ ☆ ☆ ☆
SUNDAY			☆ ☆ ☆ ☆ ☆

Notes

Mood Tracker

MONTH		WEEK	

	MONDAY	TUESDAY	WEDNESDAY	THURSDAY	FRIDAY	SATURDAY	SUNDAY
HAPPY							
NEUTRAL							
SAD							

DAY	EMOTION	WHAT HAPPENED?	DAILY SCORE
MONDAY			☆☆☆☆☆
TUESDAY			☆☆☆☆☆
WEDNESDAY			☆☆☆☆☆
THURSDAY			☆☆☆☆☆
FRIDAY			☆☆☆☆☆
SATURDAY			☆☆☆☆☆
SUNDAY			☆☆☆☆☆

Notes

Mood Tracker

MONTH							WEEK		

	MONDAY	TUESDAY	WEDNESDAY	THURSDAY	FRIDAY	SATURDAY	SUNDAY
HAPPY							
NEUTRAL							
SAD							

DAY	EMOTION	WHAT HAPPENED?	DAILY SCORE
MONDAY			☆☆☆☆☆
TUESDAY			☆☆☆☆☆
WEDNESDAY			☆☆☆☆☆
THURSDAY			☆☆☆☆☆
FRIDAY			☆☆☆☆☆
SATURDAY			☆☆☆☆☆
SUNDAY			☆☆☆☆☆

Notes

Mood Tracker

MONTH		WEEK	

HAPPY								
NEUTRAL								
SAD								
	MONDAY	TUESDAY	WEDNESDAY	THURSDAY	FRIDAY	SATURDAY	SUNDAY	

DAY	EMOTION	WHAT HAPPENED?	DAILY SCORE
MONDAY			☆ ☆ ☆ ☆ ☆
TUESDAY			☆ ☆ ☆ ☆ ☆
WEDNESDAY			☆ ☆ ☆ ☆ ☆
THURSDAY			☆ ☆ ☆ ☆ ☆
FRIDAY			☆ ☆ ☆ ☆ ☆
SATURDAY			☆ ☆ ☆ ☆ ☆
SUNDAY			☆ ☆ ☆ ☆ ☆

Notes

Mood Tracker

MONTH		WEEK	

	MONDAY	TUESDAY	WEDNESDAY	THURSDAY	FRIDAY	SATURDAY	SUNDAY
HAPPY							
NEUTRAL							
SAD							

DAY	EMOTION	WHAT HAPPENED?	DAILY SCORE
MONDAY			☆☆☆☆☆
TUESDAY			☆☆☆☆☆
WEDNESDAY			☆☆☆☆☆
THURSDAY			☆☆☆☆☆
FRIDAY			☆☆☆☆☆
SATURDAY			☆☆☆☆☆
SUNDAY			☆☆☆☆☆

Notes

Mood Tracker

MONTH						WEEK		
HAPPY								
NEUTRAL								
SAD								
	MONDAY	TUESDAY	WEDNESDAY	THURSDAY	FRIDAY	SATURDAY	SUNDAY	

DAY	EMOTION	WHAT HAPPENED?	DAILY SCORE
MONDAY			☆ ☆ ☆ ☆ ☆
TUESDAY			☆ ☆ ☆ ☆ ☆
WEDNESDAY			☆ ☆ ☆ ☆ ☆
THURSDAY			☆ ☆ ☆ ☆ ☆
FRIDAY			☆ ☆ ☆ ☆ ☆
SATURDAY			☆ ☆ ☆ ☆ ☆
SUNDAY			☆ ☆ ☆ ☆ ☆

Notes

Mood Tracker

MONTH							WEEK		

	MONDAY	TUESDAY	WEDNESDAY	THURSDAY	FRIDAY	SATURDAY	SUNDAY
HAPPY							
NEUTRAL							
SAD							

DAY	EMOTION	WHAT HAPPENED?	DAILY SCORE
MONDAY			☆ ☆ ☆ ☆ ☆
TUESDAY			☆ ☆ ☆ ☆ ☆
WEDNESDAY			☆ ☆ ☆ ☆ ☆
THURSDAY			☆ ☆ ☆ ☆ ☆
FRIDAY			☆ ☆ ☆ ☆ ☆
SATURDAY			☆ ☆ ☆ ☆ ☆
SUNDAY			☆ ☆ ☆ ☆ ☆

Notes

Mood Tracker

MONTH		WEEK	

	MONDAY	TUESDAY	WEDNESDAY	THURSDAY	FRIDAY	SATURDAY	SUNDAY
HAPPY							
NEUTRAL							
SAD							

DAY	EMOTION	WHAT HAPPENED?	DAILY SCORE
MONDAY			☆☆☆☆☆
TUESDAY			☆☆☆☆☆
WEDNESDAY			☆☆☆☆☆
THURSDAY			☆☆☆☆☆
FRIDAY			☆☆☆☆☆
SATURDAY			☆☆☆☆☆
SUNDAY			☆☆☆☆☆

Notes

Mood Tracker

MONTH							WEEK		

	MONDAY	TUESDAY	WEDNESDAY	THURSDAY	FRIDAY	SATURDAY	SUNDAY
HAPPY							
NEUTRAL							
SAD							

DAY	EMOTION	WHAT HAPPENED?	DAILY SCORE
MONDAY			☆☆☆☆☆
TUESDAY			☆☆☆☆☆
WEDNESDAY			☆☆☆☆☆
THURSDAY			☆☆☆☆☆
FRIDAY			☆☆☆☆☆
SATURDAY			☆☆☆☆☆
SUNDAY			☆☆☆☆☆

Notes

Mood Tracker

MONTH		WEEK	

	MONDAY	TUESDAY	WEDNESDAY	THURSDAY	FRIDAY	SATURDAY	SUNDAY
HAPPY							
NEUTRAL							
SAD							

DAY	EMOTION	WHAT HAPPENED?	DAILY SCORE
MONDAY			☆ ☆ ☆ ☆ ☆
TUESDAY			☆ ☆ ☆ ☆ ☆
WEDNESDAY			☆ ☆ ☆ ☆ ☆
THURSDAY			☆ ☆ ☆ ☆ ☆
FRIDAY			☆ ☆ ☆ ☆ ☆
SATURDAY			☆ ☆ ☆ ☆ ☆
SUNDAY			☆ ☆ ☆ ☆ ☆

Notes

Mood Tracker

MONTH							WEEK			

	MONDAY	TUESDAY	WEDNESDAY	THURSDAY	FRIDAY	SATURDAY	SUNDAY
HAPPY							
NEUTRAL							
SAD							

DAY	EMOTION	WHAT HAPPENED?	DAILY SCORE
MONDAY			☆☆☆☆☆
TUESDAY			☆☆☆☆☆
WEDNESDAY			☆☆☆☆☆
THURSDAY			☆☆☆☆☆
FRIDAY			☆☆☆☆☆
SATURDAY			☆☆☆☆☆
SUNDAY			☆☆☆☆☆

Notes

Mood Tracker

MONTH		WEEK	

	MONDAY	TUESDAY	WEDNESDAY	THURSDAY	FRIDAY	SATURDAY	SUNDAY
HAPPY							
NEUTRAL							
SAD							

DAY	EMOTION	WHAT HAPPENED?	DAILY SCORE
MONDAY			☆☆☆☆☆
TUESDAY			☆☆☆☆☆
WEDNESDAY			☆☆☆☆☆
THURSDAY			☆☆☆☆☆
FRIDAY			☆☆☆☆☆
SATURDAY			☆☆☆☆☆
SUNDAY			☆☆☆☆☆

Notes

Mood Tracker

MONTH		WEEK	

	MONDAY	TUESDAY	WEDNESDAY	THURSDAY	FRIDAY	SATURDAY	SUNDAY
HAPPY							
NEUTRAL							
SAD							

DAY	EMOTION	WHAT HAPPENED?	DAILY SCORE
MONDAY			☆ ☆ ☆ ☆ ☆
TUESDAY			☆ ☆ ☆ ☆ ☆
WEDNESDAY			☆ ☆ ☆ ☆ ☆
THURSDAY			☆ ☆ ☆ ☆ ☆
FRIDAY			☆ ☆ ☆ ☆ ☆
SATURDAY			☆ ☆ ☆ ☆ ☆
SUNDAY			☆ ☆ ☆ ☆ ☆

Notes

Mood Tracker

MONTH						WEEK		

HAPPY								
NEUTRAL								
SAD								
	MONDAY	TUESDAY	WEDNESDAY	THURSDAY	FRIDAY	SATURDAY	SUNDAY	

DAY	EMOTION	WHAT HAPPENED?	DAILY SCORE
MONDAY			☆☆☆☆☆
TUESDAY			☆☆☆☆☆
WEDNESDAY			☆☆☆☆☆
THURSDAY			☆☆☆☆☆
FRIDAY			☆☆☆☆☆
SATURDAY			☆☆☆☆☆
SUNDAY			☆☆☆☆☆

Notes

Mood Tracker

MONTH						WEEK			
HAPPY									
NEUTRAL									
SAD									
	MONDAY	TUESDAY	WEDNESDAY	THURSDAY	FRIDAY	SATURDAY	SUNDAY		

DAY	EMOTION	WHAT HAPPENED?	DAILY SCORE
MONDAY			☆ ☆ ☆ ☆ ☆
TUESDAY			☆ ☆ ☆ ☆ ☆
WEDNESDAY			☆ ☆ ☆ ☆ ☆
THURSDAY			☆ ☆ ☆ ☆ ☆
FRIDAY			☆ ☆ ☆ ☆ ☆
SATURDAY			☆ ☆ ☆ ☆ ☆
SUNDAY			☆ ☆ ☆ ☆ ☆

Notes

Mood Tracker

MONTH						WEEK		

	MONDAY	TUESDAY	WEDNESDAY	THURSDAY	FRIDAY	SATURDAY	SUNDAY
HAPPY							
NEUTRAL							
SAD							

DAY	EMOTION	WHAT HAPPENED?	DAILY SCORE
MONDAY			☆☆☆☆☆
TUESDAY			☆☆☆☆☆
WEDNESDAY			☆☆☆☆☆
THURSDAY			☆☆☆☆☆
FRIDAY			☆☆☆☆☆
SATURDAY			☆☆☆☆☆
SUNDAY			☆☆☆☆☆

Notes

Mood Tracker

MONTH							WEEK		

	MONDAY	TUESDAY	WEDNESDAY	THURSDAY	FRIDAY	SATURDAY	SUNDAY
HAPPY							
NEUTRAL							
SAD							

DAY	EMOTION	WHAT HAPPENED?	DAILY SCORE
MONDAY			☆☆☆☆☆
TUESDAY			☆☆☆☆☆
WEDNESDAY			☆☆☆☆☆
THURSDAY			☆☆☆☆☆
FRIDAY			☆☆☆☆☆
SATURDAY			☆☆☆☆☆
SUNDAY			☆☆☆☆☆

Notes

Mood Tracker

MONTH						WEEK			

	MONDAY	TUESDAY	WEDNESDAY	THURSDAY	FRIDAY	SATURDAY	SUNDAY
HAPPY							
NEUTRAL							
SAD							

DAY	EMOTION	WHAT HAPPENED?	DAILY SCORE
MONDAY			☆ ☆ ☆ ☆ ☆
TUESDAY			☆ ☆ ☆ ☆ ☆
WEDNESDAY			☆ ☆ ☆ ☆ ☆
THURSDAY			☆ ☆ ☆ ☆ ☆
FRIDAY			☆ ☆ ☆ ☆ ☆
SATURDAY			☆ ☆ ☆ ☆ ☆
SUNDAY			☆ ☆ ☆ ☆ ☆

Notes

Mood Tracker

MONTH						WEEK			
HAPPY									
NEUTRAL									
SAD									
	MONDAY	TUESDAY	WEDNESDAY	THURSDAY		FRIDAY	SATURDAY	SUNDAY	

DAY	EMOTION	WHAT HAPPENED?	DAILY SCORE
MONDAY			☆ ☆ ☆ ☆ ☆
TUESDAY			☆ ☆ ☆ ☆ ☆
WEDNESDAY			☆ ☆ ☆ ☆ ☆
THURSDAY			☆ ☆ ☆ ☆ ☆
FRIDAY			☆ ☆ ☆ ☆ ☆
SATURDAY			☆ ☆ ☆ ☆ ☆
SUNDAY			☆ ☆ ☆ ☆ ☆

Notes

Mood Tracker

MONTH						WEEK			
HAPPY									
NEUTRAL									
SAD									
	MONDAY	TUESDAY	WEDNESDAY	THURSDAY	FRIDAY		SATURDAY	SUNDAY	

DAY	EMOTION	WHAT HAPPENED?	DAILY SCORE
MONDAY			☆ ☆ ☆ ☆ ☆
TUESDAY			☆ ☆ ☆ ☆ ☆
WEDNESDAY			☆ ☆ ☆ ☆ ☆
THURSDAY			☆ ☆ ☆ ☆ ☆
FRIDAY			☆ ☆ ☆ ☆ ☆
SATURDAY			☆ ☆ ☆ ☆ ☆
SUNDAY			☆ ☆ ☆ ☆ ☆

Notes

Mood Tracker

MONTH						WEEK		

	MONDAY	TUESDAY	WEDNESDAY	THURSDAY	FRIDAY	SATURDAY	SUNDAY
HAPPY							
NEUTRAL							
SAD							

DAY	EMOTION	WHAT HAPPENED?	DAILY SCORE
MONDAY			☆ ☆ ☆ ☆ ☆
TUESDAY			☆ ☆ ☆ ☆ ☆
WEDNESDAY			☆ ☆ ☆ ☆ ☆
THURSDAY			☆ ☆ ☆ ☆ ☆
FRIDAY			☆ ☆ ☆ ☆ ☆
SATURDAY			☆ ☆ ☆ ☆ ☆
SUNDAY			☆ ☆ ☆ ☆ ☆

Notes

Mood Tracker

MONTH		WEEK	

	MONDAY	TUESDAY	WEDNESDAY	THURSDAY	FRIDAY	SATURDAY	SUNDAY
HAPPY							
NEUTRAL							
SAD							

DAY	EMOTION	WHAT HAPPENED?	DAILY SCORE
MONDAY			☆ ☆ ☆ ☆ ☆
TUESDAY			☆ ☆ ☆ ☆ ☆
WEDNESDAY			☆ ☆ ☆ ☆ ☆
THURSDAY			☆ ☆ ☆ ☆ ☆
FRIDAY			☆ ☆ ☆ ☆ ☆
SATURDAY			☆ ☆ ☆ ☆ ☆
SUNDAY			☆ ☆ ☆ ☆ ☆

Notes

Mood Tracker

MONTH							WEEK		
HAPPY									
NEUTRAL									
SAD									
	MONDAY	TUESDAY	WEDNESDAY	THURSDAY	FRIDAY	SATURDAY	SUNDAY		

DAY	EMOTION	WHAT HAPPENED?	DAILY SCORE
MONDAY			☆☆☆☆☆
TUESDAY			☆☆☆☆☆
WEDNESDAY			☆☆☆☆☆
THURSDAY			☆☆☆☆☆
FRIDAY			☆☆☆☆☆
SATURDAY			☆☆☆☆☆
SUNDAY			☆☆☆☆☆

Notes

Printed in Great Britain
by Amazon